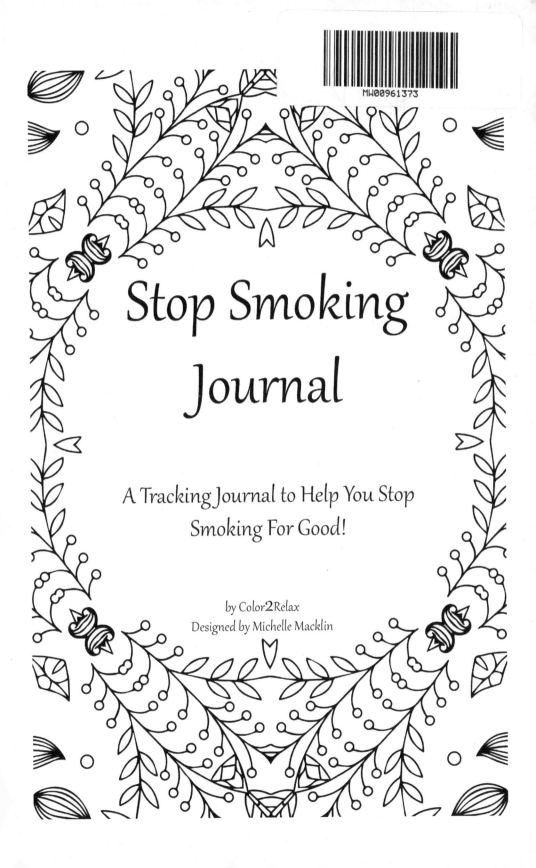

Stop Smoking

Journal

A Tracking Journal to Help You Stop Smoking For Good!

by Color2Relax
Designed by Michelle Macklin

My Dedication

To my husband, for being there through my nicotine cravings and making sure I had plenty of nicotine gum. Also, for being proud of me for finally quitting. And to my son and my grandson, the other 2 most important people in my life, I want to be around a long time for you. I wrote this journal with the knowledge I gained through my journey of finally being able to stop smoking for these 3 special guys.

Your Dedication

Use the space below to dedicate this tracking journal to the people in your life that you are quitting for, who help you quit and/or are quitting with you. The people we want to be around a long time for can be great motivators to quit smoking for good.

_____

_____

_____

_____

_____

I Will Stop Smoking On This Date

_____

Research shows that picking a date to quit smoking 2 weeks ahead of time increases your chances of quitting for good. Whether you decide to quit today or 2 weeks from today, write the date you will become smoke free in the space above. Writing down the date is an important first step to stop smoking,

5 Steps to Quit For Life

1. Quit at your own pace.
2. Conquer your urges to smoke
3. Use medications, patches, gum or lozenges
4. Control your environment
5. Get social support

Why I Want To Quit Smoking

_____

_____

_____

_____

_____

_____

_____

_____

_____

_____

Fill out during your 2 weeks before quitting. Use a different color for each activity, mood and need rating. Color in the boxes describing each cigarette you smoke. This tracking diary will help you realize your smoking triggers so you can avoid them or stop them before they become a problem after you quit.

MY SMOKING DIARY

Time	Activity							Mood							Other Activities, Feelings - Describe	Need Rating		
	Food	Alcohol	Coffee	Friends	Family	Driving	Angry	Happy	Sad	Bored	Relaxed	Tired			Low	Medium	High

Color

Activity
Food _____
Alcohol _____
Coffee _____
Friends _____
Family _____
Driving _____
Angry _____
Happy _____
Sad _____
Bored _____
Relaxed _____
Tired _____
Low _____
Medium _____
High _____

MY SMOKING DIARY

Time	Activity							Mood						Other Activities, Feelings - Describe	Need Rating		
	Food	Alcohol	Coffee	Friends	Family	Driving	Angry	Happy	Sad	Bored	Relaxed	Tired		Low	Medium	High

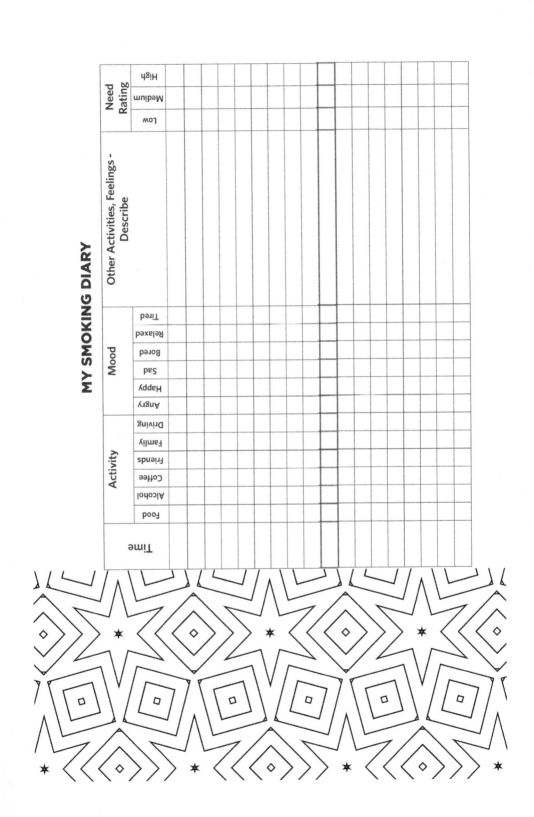

MY SMOKING DIARY

Time	Activity							Mood							Other Activities, Feelings - Describe	Need Rating		
	Food	Alcohol	Coffee	Friends	Family	Driving	Angry	Happy	Sad	Bored	Relaxed	Tired		Low	Medium	High

Color

Activity
Food
Alcohol
Coffee
Friends
Family
Driving
Angry
Happy
Sad
Bored
Relaxed
Tired
Low
Medium
High

MY SMOKING DIARY

Time	Activity						Mood						Other Activities, Feelings - Describe	Need Rating		
	Food	Alcohol	Coffee	Friends	Family	Driving	Angry	Happy	Sad	Bored	Relaxed	Tired		Low	Medium	High

MY SMOKING DIARY

Time	Activity							Mood						Other Activities, Feelings - Describe	Need Rating		
	Food	Alcohol	Coffee	Friends	Family	Driving	Angry	Happy	Sad	Bored	Relaxed	Tired			Low	Medium	High

Color _____

Activity
Food
Alcohol
Coffee
Friends
Family
Driving
Angry
Happy
Sad
Bored
Relaxed
Tired
Low
Medium
High

MY SMOKING DIARY

Time	Activity						Mood						Other Activities, Feelings - Describe	Need Rating		
	Food	Alcohol	Coffee	Friends	Family	Driving	Angry	Happy	Sad	Bored	Relaxed	Tired		Low	Medium	High

2 Weeks Before My Quit Date....

1. Think about things you like to do other than smoking..._____

_____

_____

_____

_____

2. Fill out the Track Your Smoking worksheet if you havent already...

3. Become active at least 3 times a week. If you have health problems or haven't exercised in awhile, talk to your doctor first...

4. Decide how you will deal with urges to smoke..._____

_____

_____

Tips for this week:

*Delay your first cigarette of the day for as long as you can. Then try to smoke only one per hour.

*Put your cigarettes somewhere that makes you have to get up to get one. For example, in a cabinet, in your car, etc. Don't let it be easy to grab one and have it lit before you know it.

*Before every cigarette, think about why you are smoking it. Is it a craving for it, or is it a habit because you are on the phone , driving, or doing some other activity.

How have you changed your smoking habit this week..._____

_____

_____

_____

_____

_____

_____

_____

_____

_____

1 Week Before My Quit Date....

1. Stop smoking in your car and your home...

2. Practice quitting for a few hours at a time. These are called "mini quits" and are useful to allow you to start coping with the urges to smoke....

3. If your doctor has prescribed you medication, start taking it this week so it will be in your system on quit day...

4. Start gathering your supplies such as nicotine gum, lozenges or patches, water, straws or stir sticks, celery, carrots, healthy snacks and anything you think will help you keep your hands busy and get over a craving...

Tips for this week...

    * This week you should start finding ways to change your daily routine. Get up later so you don't have time to smoke, drink tea instead of coffee, etc.

    * Get adult coloring books, puzzle books, a new book to read, etc so you will have things to do. Boredom is a huge smoking trigger.

    * Join support groups on Facebook, Twitter, or in your home town. It can be helpful to talk to others who are quitting.

What did you do this week to prepare for your quit date:

_____

_____

_____

_____

_____

_____

_____

1 Day Before My Quit Date....

1. Wash the ashtray in your car. Fill it with sunflower seeds or flowers.

2. Review the instructions on your nicotine replacement therapy. Make sure you know the right way to use them.

3. Decide how you will manage stress. Try deep breathing exercises, meditation or adult coloring books.

4. Before you go to bed, throw away all lighters and cigarettes Wash ashtrays and put them away or get rid of them.

Tips for today...

* It is easier to quit smoking if you wake up tomorrow and don't smoke, rather than quitting in the middle of the day. This way you sleep through the worst cravings.

*Start brushing your teeth right after eating each meal. This gets you away from the table and gives you something to focus on instead of smoking.

*Make a list of rewards for staying smoke free for 1 week, 1 month, and 1 year. The money you save from not smoking can pay for your rewards.

1 Week Reward_____

1 Month Reward_____

1 Year Reward_____

My First Day Smoke Free....

Congratulations on waking up a non-smoker today!

You will be surprised at how easy today will be. This was the easiest day for me because I had all the supplies I needed. It was easiest for my husband because he didn't have to run to the store at 11pm to get my nicotine gum I had forgotten to pick up that day. The most important thing to remember today is you have prepared for this, you have all your supplies and you know how to beat your urges to smoke when your triggers pop up. Make sure you get out of bed quickly and attack the day! While you will think a lot about cigarettes today, you can smile knowing that they do not have a hold over you anymore. When the craving tries to overcome you just think, you have already went hours without a cigarette and if you decide to have just one more, that cigarette will only help your craving for an hour or so and then you will want another one. "Just one more" is not worth erasing all the time you went without one today. Use your nicotine replacement and/or do an activity that makes smoking impossible. It will get easier. You can do this!

Nicotine Withdrawal Symptoms:

Urge to smoke	Increased appetite
Depressed mood	Restlessness
Anxiety	Difficulty concentrating
Irritability	Frustration
Insomnia	Anger

Speak with your doctor if any of the symptoms become severe. Also be aware of any side effects of prescribed medications.

What helped you beat your urges to smoke today the most?_____

_____

_____

What helped the least, or didn't help at all?_____

_____

_____

When did you have the worst urges to smoke?

_____

_____

_____

Which withdrawal symptoms did you notice? ____

_____

_____

_____

How do you feel at the end of the day?_____

_____

_____

_____

DATE:_____

24 Hours after quitting your blood pressure and pulse rate may drop

Did you have more or less urges to smoke today?_____
_____
_____

What helped you get through your cravings to smoke?
_____
_____
_____

How do you feel today?_____
_____
_____
_____
_____
_____
_____
_____
_____

Did you smoke today? Why or why not? _____

_____

_____

_____

_____

_____

_____

Color and relax...

DATE:_____

48 Hours after quitting your nerve endings start
to regrow and your ability to smell and taste will
improve

Did you have more or less urges to smoke today?_____
_____

_____

What helped you get through your cravings to smoke?
_____

_____

_____

How do you feel today?_____
_____

_____

_____

_____

_____

_____

_____

Did you smoke today? Why or why not? _____

_____

_____

_____

_____

_____

_____

Color and relax...

DATE:_____

3 days after quitting your symptoms of chemical withdrawal are beginning to decrease.

Did you have more or less urges to smoke today?_____
_____
_____

What helped you get through your cravings to smoke?
_____
_____
_____

How do you feel today?_____
_____
_____
_____
_____
_____
_____
_____

Did you smoke today? Why or why not? _____

_____

_____

_____

_____

_____

Color and relax...

DATE:_____

4 days after quitting your breathing is becoming
easier as your lung functions begin to improve.

Did you have more or less urges to smoke today?_____
_____

_____

What helped you get through your cravings to smoke?

_____

_____

_____

How do you feel today?_____

_____

_____

_____

_____

_____

_____

_____

Did you smoke today? Why or why not? _____
_____
_____
_____
_____
_____
_____

Color and relax...

DATE:_____

Get Rid Of The Smoke Smell: Steam clean your furniture and carpets. Wash any curtains in your home, your clothes and all your bed linens.

Did you have more or less urges to smoke today?_____

_____

_____

What helped you get through your cravings to smoke?

_____

_____

_____

How do you feel today?_____

_____

_____

_____

_____

_____

_____

_____

Did you smoke today? Why or why not? _____
_____
_____
_____
_____
_____
_____

Color and relax...

DATE:_____

Vigorous exercise can provide the dopamine release
you used to get from cigarettes. Staying active will
also speed up your body's self-repair process.

Did you have more or less urges to smoke today?_____
_____

_____

What helped you get through your cravings to smoke?
_____

_____

_____

How do you feel today?_____
_____

_____

_____

_____

_____

_____

_____

Did you smoke today? Why or why not? _____

_____

_____

_____

_____

_____

_____

Color and relax...

DATE:_____

Consider taking up a new hobby such as painting, pottery, or creative writing to take your mind off smoking. Cooking will take advantage of your improved sense of smell and taste.

Did you have more or less urges to smoke today?_____

_____

_____

What helped you get through your cravings to smoke?

_____

_____

_____

How do you feel today?_____

_____

_____

_____

_____

_____

_____

_____

Did you smoke today? Why or why not? _____

_____

_____

_____

_____

_____

Color and relax...

DATE:_____

Its important to find new ways to relax and calm yourself without nicotine. Buy a stress relief ball, silly putty or an adult coloring book to begin new, healthy stress relieving habits.

Did you have more or less urges to smoke today?_____

_____

_____

What helped you get through your cravings to smoke?

_____

_____

_____

How do you feel today?_____

_____

_____

_____

_____

_____

_____

_____

Did you smoke today? Why or why not? _____

_____

_____

_____

_____

_____

_____

Color and relax...

DATE:_____

Nicotine suppresses the effects of caffiene, so after you quit, coffee and soda will have a stronger effect on you. It increases your heart rate and makes dealing with stress more difficult.

Did you have more or less urges to smoke today?_____
_____

_____

What helped you get through your cravings to smoke?
_____

_____

_____

How do you feel today?_____
_____

_____

_____

_____

_____

_____

_____

Did you smoke today? Why or why not? _____

_____

_____

_____

_____

_____

_____

Color and relax...

DATE:_____

Water will speed up the nicotine detox. Water can also help ease your cough by making it easier for your lungs to clear out the mucus and it will combat your increased appetite.

Did you have more or less urges to smoke today?_____

_____

_____

What helped you get through your cravings to smoke?

_____

_____

_____

How do you feel today?_____

_____

_____

_____

_____

_____

_____

_____

Did you smoke today? Why or why not? _____

_____

_____

_____

_____

_____

_____

Color and relax...

DATE:_____

Deep breathing will fight cravings since it will relax
and calm you. The extra oxygen will help with the
headaches. If you have smoked for a long time, it will
release the residual nicotine in your lungs.

Did you have more or less urges to smoke today?_____

_____

_____

What helped you get through your cravings to smoke?

_____

_____

_____

How do you feel today?_____

_____

_____

_____

_____

_____

_____

_____

Did you smoke today? Why or why not? _____

_____

_____

_____

_____

_____

Color and relax...

DATE:_____

You may cough more after you quit smoking. This is
the lungs cleaning themselves. The coughing
should drastically decrease within 9 months.

Did you have more or less urges to smoke today?_____
_____

_____

What helped you get through your cravings to smoke?
_____

_____

_____

How do you feel today?_____

_____

_____

_____

_____

_____

_____

_____

Did you smoke today? Why or why not? _____

_____

_____

_____

_____

_____

_____

Color and relax...

DATE:_____

The yellow stains on your teeth will fade after you
quit smoking. Your lips will look better as you are
less likely to have burns or mouth sores.

Did you have more or less urges to smoke today?_____
_____
_____

What helped you get through your cravings to smoke?
_____
_____
_____

How do you feel today?_____
_____
_____
_____
_____
_____
_____
_____

Did you smoke today? Why or why not? _____

_____

_____

_____

_____

_____

_____

Color and relax...

DATE:_____

2-4 weeks after quitting the psychological effects
of withdrawal stop. You should not have any
nicotine withdrawal symptoms after 4 weeks.

Did you have more or less urges to smoke today?_____
_____
_____

What helped you get through your cravings to smoke?
_____
_____
_____

How do you feel today?_____
_____
_____
_____
_____
_____
_____
_____

Did you smoke today? Why or why not? _____

_____

_____

_____

_____

_____

_____

Color and relax...

DATE:_____

1 year after quitting the risk of heart attack, stroke and coronary heart disease have dropped to half that of a smoker.

Did you have more or less urges to smoke today?_____

_____

_____

What helped you get through your cravings to smoke?

_____

_____

_____

How do you feel today?_____

_____

_____

_____

_____

_____

_____

_____

Did you smoke today? Why or why not? _____

_____

_____

_____

_____

_____

Color and relax...

DATE: _____

It has been over a month since your quit date. Take a
moment to write about how you feel, physically and
mentally. _____

_____

_____

_____

_____

_____

_____

_____

How has quitting smoking changed your life? _____

_____

_____

_____

_____

_____

_____

CHECK OFF THE BENEFITS YOU FEEL IN YOUR NEW SMOKE-FREE LIFE.

☐ I can breathe better

☐ I have an improved sense of smell

☐ I smell better

☐ My food tastes better

☐ I don't cough anymore

☐ I don't wheeze anymore

☐ I have more energy

☐ I feel more in control

☐ I feel a sense of freedom

☐ I have saved money

☐ My house is cleaner

☐ I feel good about myself

☐ I sleep better

☐ Add your own:

_____

_____

_____

DATE:_____

Keep writing in your journal as long as it helps you

_____

_____

_____

_____

_____

_____

_____

_____

_____

_____

_____

_____

_____

_____

_____

_____

_____

DATE:_____

DATE:_____

DATE:_____

DATE:_____

DATE:_____

DATE:_____

DATE:_____

DATE:_____

DATE:_____

DATE:_____

DATE:_____

DATE:_____

DATE:_____

DATE:_____

DATE:_____

_____
_____
_____
_____
_____
_____
_____
_____
_____
_____
_____
_____
_____
_____
_____
_____
_____
_____
_____
_____

DATE:_____

Made in the USA
Middletown, DE
24 January 2021